GUIDE

TO THE

YUKON GOLD FIELDS

WHERE THEY ARE AND HOW TO REACH THEM

By V. WILSON

With Maps and Many Illustrations

SEATTLE
THE CALVERT COMPANY
1895

COPYRIGHT, 1895, BY V. WILSON.

CONTENTS.

	PAGE
Introduction	13
Where and What to Buy for an Outfit	17
List of Provisions	18
The Start	20
Lake Lindeman	20
Whip-sawing	21
Lake Bennett	22
Tagish Lake	22
Caribou Crossing	23
Windy Arm	23
Tagish House	24
Lake Marsh	25
Martins' Nests	25
Salmon	25
Grand Canyon	26
White Horse Rapids	28
Proposed Tramway Route	29
Tahkeena River	30
Lake Labarge	30
Hootalinqua River	31
Big Salmon River	32
Little Salmon River	32
Five Fingers	33
Rink Rapids	33
Old Fort Selkirk	33
White River	34
Volcanic Ash Deposits	35
Stewart River	36
Sixty Mile Creek	36
Indian Creek	36
Clondike River	37
Forty Mile Creek	37
Miller Creek	38
Freighting	39
Glacier Creek	39
Prospecting and Mining	39
Bed-Rock Creek	40
Bald Hills	41
Forty Mile Post	41
Dogs	42
Fort Cudahy	43
Coal Creek	44
Circle City	44
Birch Creek	45

TABLE OF CONTENTS

Preacher Creek	46
Yukon Flats	46
Fossils	47
Lower Ramparts	48
Muklukyeto City	49
Koyukuk River	49
Lower River Natives	49
St. Michaels Island	50
Navigation of the Yukon	51
Taku Route	52
White Pass	53
Chilkoot Pass	53
Chilkat Pass	54
Possible Railroad Route	54
Resources	55
Copper	55
Iron and Coal	55
Platinum	55
Game	55
Moose	55
Caribou	56
Barren Land Caribou	56
Arctic Reindeer	56
Bear	57
Mountain Goat	58
Mountain Sheep	58
Lynx	58
Wolves	59
Wolverine	59
Fish	59
Discovery of Gold in the Yukon Basin	60
Source of the Yukon	61
Climate	62
Winter Clothes	63
New Discovery at Cook Inlet	64
The Yukon River	64
Indians Along the Yukon	66
Purchase of Alaska	68
Area and Extent	69
Juneau	69
Douglass Island	70
Gold Dust	71
Sale on Bed-Rock	71
Miners' Laws	71
A Model Firm	72
A New Steamboat Line	72

TABLE OF DISTANCES.

The following distances from Juneau are taken from Ogilvie's survey as far as it has been made; the others are according to the best authorities to be found.

	MILES
Haines Mission	80
Taiya	100
Head of Canoe Navigation, Taiya River	106
Summit Chilkoot Pass	114¾
Head of Lake Lindeman	123½
Foot of Lake Lindeman	127½
Head of Lake Bennett	128¼
Foot of Lake Bennett	153¼
Caribou Crossing	156½
Foot of Tagish Lake	173¼
Head of Lake Marsh	178¼
Foot of Lake Marsh	197¼
Head of Canyon	223
Foot of Canyon	223¾
Head of White Horse Rapids	225¼
Tahkeena River	240
Head of Lake Labarge	235
Foot of Lake Labarge	284
Hootalinqua River	316
Big Salmon River	349
Little Salmon River	385½
Five Finger Rapids	444
Rink Rapids	450
Pelly River	503½
White River	599½
Stewart River	609
Sixty Mile Post	629
Fort Reliance	682½
Forty Mile Post	728
Fort Cudahy	728¼
Moose Creek on Forty Mile River	754
Head of Miller Creek	788

PREFACE.

The much felt want of definite information concerning the Yukon gold-fields and how to reach them, and the almost total absence of anything like a good guide-book to that region, at a time when the eyes of nearly the entire mining world are turned in that direction, have prompted the author to place before the public the many facts he has learned by personal observation and diligent inquiry of those who have spent many years in that region. No attempt has been made to put forth a literary production. A statement of facts in simple language has been followed. It has been left to some tourist of the future to give to the public a volume embellished with rhetorical figure and lofty description. This volume is intended for a hand-book to be used by everyone, tourist, prospector and miner, for ready reference, telling how to get into the Yukon basin, how to get out of it and what has been found there.

It is not only the purpose of these pages to give such information as will prove of benefit to those who may undertake the trip, but also to discourage those unfit to encounter the hardships and correctly to inform those who have been led to believe that nuggets could be gathered from the beds of streams like pebbles.

The illustrations are from photographs and are the only ones ever successfully taken of the upper river and mines, while the maps are drawn from personal observation and information given by miners.

In concluding these prefatory remarks I wish to acknowledge with gratitude my indebtedness to Billy Lloyd, Frank Knight, Frank Densmore, Mr. Cornell and others, as well as to Pither, an Indian, who has traveled extensively through the Yukon basin.

V. W.

MEMOIR.

Soon after the notes from which this work was compiled were handed to the publishers, the author was taken seriously ill, and just at the hour the book comes from the press there comes also the sad news of the author's death. "Strange indeed," one would say, "that a man of such a strong physique, possessed of an iron will, should give way to the ravages of fever." But not so strange to one who knew the suffering and hardships encountered and endured by Mr. Wilson during his voyage of exploration the past year in Alaska. I met him on the morning of June 15th at the head waters of the Yukon River, and was with him during the greater part of the four thousand mile journey. While scarcely thirty years of age, he was a natural explorer and always seemed as much at home with the Indians among rocky fastnesses of the North as he would be in the midst of the æsthetic surroundings of his father's home in Maine. He could transform hardships into pleasures; in the presence of danger, always calm and deliberate, a keen observer, joyful spirited, never uttering a murmur about the heavy pack upon his back while making long journeys across the mountains but would revel in the beauty and grandeur of his surroundings. He was a man of fine abilities, a good conversationalist with pleasing manner, a strong personality, very kind and genial under all circumstances, making friends wherever he went.

His life has been sacrificed to gain and give to the world the valuable information contained in the following pages, and in this sense it has been sacrificed for others. Having traveled the same route as the author, I can confidently say that this guide will prove invaluable to anyone going to Alaska, and in the memory of those who follow its directions will be erected an enduring monument to him who died in the hope of a life everlasting beyond the confines of mortality.

J. O. HESTWOOD.

Seattle, January 5, 1895.

MIDNIGHT AT LAKE BENNETT

INTRODUCTORY.

The rush to the Yukon last spring saw many prospectors in the field with the most promising results. Many new creeks were discovered of great extent and richness, and all the old mines yielded better results than ever before.

No creek in the entire basin which was prospected with any degree of precision failed to show at least a color.

The estimated amount of gold taken out of the country last year has been placed as high as one million dollars, and while this is highly improbable, the many who have returned with amounts varying from five to thirty-five thousand dollars prove beyond a doubt that the country is one of great richness.

With these facts fresh before the public, at a time when the brawn and muscle of our great nation is almost at a standstill, it may reasonably be expected that many will turn their attention in this direction, and it is therefore the purpose of these pages to give such information as will be of benefit to those who undertake the trip.

The Chilkoot pass is the only route used to any extent at present by the miners, and is the shortest portage from salt water to the navigable waters of the Yukon. This route leads over the Chilkoot pass down the lakes to Lewis river, thence down the Yukon to the mines at different points on that river.

The trip is one of difficulties which will tax the endurance and nerve of the most hardy, and only such men can reasonably expect to succeed. For only with the most incessant toil, such as packing provisions over pathless mountains, towing a heavy boat against a five to an eight mile current, over battered boulders, digging in the bottomless frost, sleeping where night overtakes, fighting gnats and mosquitos by the million, shooting seething canyons and rapids and enduring for seven long months a relentless cold which never rises above zero and frequently falls to 80 below—any man physically endowed to overcome these obstacles who will go there for a few years, can by strict attention to business make a good stake with the possibilities of a fortune.

The climate is one unequalled for health, the summer months

are delightful, game is plenty in season, and the winters, while cold, are healthy and help to recuperate the lost vitality from the incessant toil of summer.

The next few years will see wagon roads and trails through the Coast range, steamers on the lakes and upper river, and the whole of the vast upper country will be made accessible to the miner. Then hundreds will flock there and ten years will see a population of one hundred thousand people in the Yukon basin.

Then its vast richness will become the by-word of the world, for it is a poor man's country—nature has stored her treasure in a safe of ice with a time lock which only opens in the long sunny days of summer.

Hydraulic mining is made impossible owing to lack of water, for only the glacial drip of the hills is accessible in the gulches which carry the most gold. This will make its period of productiveness much greater, while capital will find lucrative investments in the rich lodes of gold, iron, coal and copper, and in the bars of the rivers which have become no longer useful to the pan or cradle in the hands of the miner. All along the whole route from the Coast range down to old Fort Yukon, the close observer can see vast treasures in the mountains, coal, marble and copper, only waiting for the country to develop to such an extent as to bring them within reach of the outside world.

The country south of the Pelly river is quite well timbered. It is a good grazing country; all the hardy vegetables grow well and even wheat ripens.

It is a fine game and fish country. Bear of several varieties, moose, caribou, wolves and many fur-bearing animals abound. It is doubtless the greatest country in the world for the silver and the black fox. The rivers and lakes are teeming with many varieties of fish, while grouse and rabbits are numerous along the shore. Water fowl of many kinds are plenty and their long sojourning in these inland waters gives to their flesh a flavor, which, although high and gamy, never acquires that repulsive, fishy taste so universal to the fowls of this coast.

When once this country is made accessible from the Sound points by proper transportation facilities, it can be reached in ten days. Then it will become one of the greatest tourist countries of the world, for where is grander scenery, a more beautiful climate, or a more favored spot, than is this lake country during three months in summer? The shores are bordered by strips of green meadow, bedecked with wild roses and an endless variety of flowers of the most delicate tints, while terraced, open and timbered slopes stretch away to high mountains which in turn are backed by snow-capped peaks.

During the whole summer scarcely any rain falls, with the exception of an occasional thunder-shower; the sun is seldom lost sight of except for a brief period at night.

Within three years it will be possible to leave Seattle in spring, work in the mines all summer and return in the fall. Then the importance of these vast gold fields will come to be realized, and in the near future the word Yukon will associate itself so closely with that of gold, that its mere mention will convey impressions of an Eldorado, rivaling that of fable.

THE GUIDE BOOK

TO

THE GOLD-FIELDS OF THE YUKON

WHERE AND WHAT TO BUY FOR AN OUTFIT.

In deciding to make the trip, the greatest considerations are how long it is necessary to stay, how much money is needed and the results to be attained. The answer to the last question, here as in all other countries, depends entirely on the man.

The country is of such extent and richness that the possibilities are unlimited, and a good rustler cannot fail to make a good round sum if he will stay at least three years. Little can be accomplished in less time than that, unless one is indeed lucky.

A good part of the first season will be consumed in reaching the mines; then, if a claim is located, only the preliminary work can be done. The second year it can be well opened up and in all probability some money made. The third year usually gives the promised results. I would advise no man to start with less than four hundred dollars, as the expense of reaching the mines is considerable and the companies doing business there refuse absolutely to give credit, as they can sell all their goods for ready cash. Some men who wanted to remain were obliged to leave the country last year on that account.

The companies doing business there have in the past helped such men out of the country, but in the future, owing to this fact's becoming generally known, they will refuse to give any assistance whatever. This decision, I understand, they will advertise extensively this coming spring.

Having decided to make the trip the outfit needed for the long journey down the river to the mines is of the greatest consideration. The actual necessities for the trip are given in a list below. The supply of clothes should be governed by ones needs, taste and purse. It is also desirable to take along a small, well-filled medicine chest.

The outfit proper can be bought to better advantage in Juneau than elsewhere, for the large outfitting establishments there have learned from long experience what is most needed and their prices will compare favorably with prices on the Sound. One may be sure of getting just what is needed without any extra weight, which is of the greatest importance, as many hard portages are to be encountered on the trip.

LIST OF PROVISIONS FOR ONE MAN ONE MONTH:

Twenty pounds of flour with baking powder	1 bean pot
12 pounds of bacon	2 plates
6 pounds of beans	1 drinking cup
5 pounds of dried fruits	1 tea pot
3 pounds of dessicated vegetables	1 knife and fork
4 pounds of butter	1 large and 1 small cooking pan
5 pounds of sugar	**TOOLS FOR BOAT BUILDING.**
4 cans of milk	1 jack plane
1 pound of tea	1 whip saw
3 pounds of coffee	1 hand saw
2 pounds of salt	1 rip saw
5 pounds of corn meal	1 draw knife
Pepper	1 ax
Matches	1 hatchet
Mustard	1 pocket rule
Cooking utensils and dishes	6 pounds of assorted nails
1 frying pan	3 pounds of oakum
1 water kettle	5 pounds of pitch
Tent	50 feet of ⅝ rope
Yukon stove	Mosquito netting
2 pair good blankets	1 pair crag-proof hip boots
1 rubber blanket	Snow-glasses
	Medicines

The above is the list of provisions generally taken by miners and is sufficient for one man for one month. The length of the trip

SCENES NEAR LAKE BENNETT
Building Boat   Camp Life   Whip-sawing

will be regulated by the season of starting and the amount necessary for the entire trip easily ascertained.

That is, if parties decide to do their own transporting over the divide they should start not later than the first of April—better by the middle of March—then they can sleigh their outfit over the summit and down the lakes to where suitable boat timber can be found. If the start is made by the middle of March, the whole distance of the lakes can be accomplished by sleigh, a boat built and the start made down the river as soon as it breaks up, which is much earlier than on the lakes. By doing this the mines may be reached four weeks earlier than by building the boat at the head of the lakes and waiting for the ice to leave.

The trip down the lakes by sleigh is usually exciting; a large sail is fixed to the sleigh and long distances are made in a single day over the hard snow and ice. If the start is made later than the last of April it is customary to hire the packing done by the Indians, who pack to Lake Lindeman, a distance of twenty-four miles, for fourteen dollars per hundred. There is no timber on the lake suitable for boat building, and a raft will have to be made to take the outfit to where better timber can be found.

A good rifle of large calibre should be taken along, as large game is plenty. Also a trout line for grayling which can be caught with a small black fly at the mouth of small streams and at the foot of rapids all along below the lakes. A good pair of snow-glasses should not be overlooked, as attacks of snow blindness are only thus prevented in crossing the summit, and nothing proves more painful. In several cases it has actually driven miners insane, and often delays those, not thus provided, for days and even weeks. E. Valentine, of Juneau, keeps a special glass at a small cost, adapted to the trip. It is customary to take mining tools from Juneau for prospecting along the trip or for any stop that might be made on the way down the river.

One man should not attempt to make the trip alone, and where four or five go in one party one tent, stove and set of tools will do for all, thus making the outfit of each lighter and also lessening the cost. One of each party should have some knowledge of boat building; the boats mostly in use are the long, double-end bateau, but for a party of five or six a scow of good depth will be found convenient and roomy, will run bad water and is easily built.

THE START.

OVER THE SUMMIT AND DOWN LAKE LINDEMAN.

After the outfit is completed the trip to *Taiya, one hundred miles distant from Juneau and the head of steamboat navigation, will be made on the *Scavlin* or *Rustler*, the charge being ten dollars for one man and outfit.

At Taiya the actual journey begins. If the trip is made by sleighs the parties usually do their own work, but if the snow and ice have left the canyon then the outfit will have to be packed to Lake Lindeman. Indian packers can be found without much difficulty to pack for the regulation price, fourteen dollars per hundred pounds, the distance being about twenty-four miles. Canoes can be used for some six miles up the Taiya river to the canyon where the trail leads up the rugged sides along a timbered shelf overlooking the canyon until Sheep Camp is reached; this is practically the timber line, and from here to the summit the trail leads up a narrow and precipitous defile. The summit is fifteen miles distant and thirty-five hundred feet above tide water.

Many glaciers are passed in the fifteen miles. After leaving the summit there is a sheer descent of five hundred feet to the bed of Crater lake. This lake retains snow and ice all the year and undoubtedly occupies an extinct crater. The water has cut a small canyon down the mountain side which should be followed to Lake Lindeman.

LAKE LINDEMAN.

THE FIRST NAVIGABLE WATERS RUNNING INTO THE YUKON.

Around the lake the timber is nearly all burned off, there being none suitable for boat building. Here a raft should be made with a deck of small poles some foot or more above the body, thus preventing the waves from wetting the outfit which should be protected by water tight sacks either of oilskin or canvas. The dried timber makes good material for rafts, but as it is small a great deal will necessarily have to be used. Lake Lindeman occupies the terminus of the same valley occupied by Lake Bennett, and is separated from the latter by a short portage of three-fourths of a mile the fall in this distance being about twenty feet. The stream con-

---

*Spelled *Dyea* in advertisements and by the white inhabitants.

of the manner in which the pit should be built, showing the log blocked in place so as to rest firmly on the cross pieces.

It should first be slabbed after ascertaining how wide a board it will make. The ends are squared and a plumb line made down the center of each end, then half the width of the board to be sawed will be laid off each side of this center line and a line struck from end to end on top, the log turned over and lined on the under side. This will bring the lumber sawed as nearly out of the center as possible. Then turn it back in place and the top line will be found directly above the bottom one. After the slabs are taken off and the log turned so the slabbed side will rest on the cross pieces, make a plumb-line again at right angles with the slab, then mark off as many boards each side of this line as the log will make and line them top and bottom. The ends may be all sawed up to the cross pieces and the log moved one way or the other until the scarf will admit the saw.

After the lumber is sawed it will probably need some dressing. The slabs will answer for oars and timbers for the boat, which will be built according to the needs of the party.

LAKE BENNETT AND TAGISH LAKE.

Lake Bennett has an average breadth of one mile with an extreme breadth of five, and is twenty-six miles long. In running this lake on raft or in boat much care should be taken, as strong winds are sure to be encountered. These are noticed most at the upper end of the lake, which occupies virtually a large canyon. The winds are always in the south and are caused by the hot air of the inland valleys, which in turn is supplemented by the cooler air of the coast, rushing inland over the low passes and down the lakes. High mountains rise abruptly on either side making it exceedingly difficult to find a landing for some miles down the lake.

Lake Bennett thus forms a funnel for the Chilkoot pass, while Windy Arm is continually swept by the currents of the White pass. These winds die out in the latter part of the night and early morning, but as the sun's warm rays heat the inland valleys their force increases until they reach the dignity of a high gale, which sometimes delays the boatmen for days. Few have ever crossed the Windy Arm without having good cause to remember it.

A large arm comes into Bennett from the west which Schwatka called Wheeton river. Lake Bennett is surrounded by lofty mountains, some reaching a height of eight thousand feet.

About five miles down the lake the formation changes from the Coast range granite to that of limestone, the change forming a definite line which crosses the lake obliquely and can be followed for miles. The formation for miles north of this is carboniferous with croppings of coal and iron. Volcanic material is found here as well as along the entire length of the route. The lower end of Bennett broadens out into a beautiful valley which stretches away to the north. It proved a great disappointment when we learned that our course turned abruptly around the mountain to the east instead of following this inviting looking country, which we had felt sure was the course of the river.

Low-terraced, grassy and open-timbered slopes here skirt the lakes and foothills of the higher mountains as well as all the lakes below. The climate is quite dry, and little rain falls except an occasional thunder-shower. The sun is warm and the clouds fleecy, but the snow-capped peaks always give the air those cool, bracing propensities which prove so disastrous to the bacon and beans.

CARIBOU CROSSING.

The connecting waters between Lake Bennett and Tagish lake constitute what is called Caribou crossing. Here there is a slight current while the channel is very crooked and shallow. This is one of the crossings used by the bands of barren-land caribou in their migration south in the fall and return in the spring.

To the west a number of low, irregular sand hills border the crossing and Tagish lake, extending around the broad valley at the north end of Lake Bennett. Along the hills the trail followed by the bands of caribou can be traced for miles.

WINDY ARM.

Two miles from Caribou crossing the Windy Arm enters Tagish lake. There are three islands at its mouth, while beyond are high mountains of limestone and marble. The marble is of a fine quality and curiously marked with gray and black, which would undoubtedly give a beautiful effect when polished. Beyond these cliffs a dome-shaped mountain can be seen standing out alone and of very defined form; it appears to be of massive limestone. On the west the country becomes better timbered and a few miles further the lake arm comes in from the south-east. This appears to be the main lake, it being much the larger, occupying a large, broad valley as far as the eye can reach.

I was informed by an Indian that it runs back three days' journey or forty miles, also that other lakes lie beyond and that the connections have no currents; thus it becomes impossible to tell the extent of navigable waters of this wonderful lake system, they not having been explored. These lakes lie at an elevation of about twenty-two hundred feet above sea level and represent hundreds of miles of navigable waters surrounded by a good grazing country, rich in minerals and good timber, while all the hardy vegetables grow well. A large fish of symmetrical lines is found here that rises readily to a troll and has every appearance of the landlocked salmon. It is of salmon color but turns white as soon as placed on the fire, and is almost tasteless when cooked.

Tagish lake is connected with Lake Marsh by a wide reach of river with a sluggish current. The banks are bordered by terraced and open wooded slopes and the valley is broad especially to the west.

The timber here is mostly cottonwood and white spruce. This piece of river is five miles long and in some places very shallow, like the lower end of Tagish lake. The water in this lake is clear and covers the hard, gravelly bottom to a depth of four or five feet, for nearly its entire lower end, which is three miles wide and five miles long.

TAGISH HOUSE.

On this piece of river is located the famous Tagish house where councils of war and the yearly festivals are held. These buildings are the only permanent buildings seen in all the country above Pelly river.

It was here war was declared years ago on the Coast Indians, which resulted so disastrously to the Sticks. These houses are kept up by annual renovation. Here also is one of their burying grounds and crematories.

LAKE MARSH.

Lake Marsh is twenty miles in length, with an average width of more than two miles. It occupies a notably broad valley, while to the east a high and well defined range of mountains stands out prominently. To the west the country is rolling, except in the vicinity of the lake, which is bordered by meadows. Many wild fowl were seen here. Away to the west a broken range of mountains reaches a greater height than those to the east. Here we saw the first snow since the high peaks about Bennett disappeared from view.

At the lower end of the lake a large island stands just above the outlet and the McClintock river enters here, draining a broad valley to the east. This river cannot be of any considerable size as the Hootalinqua is at no great distance.

Here huge piles of driftwood, the first of any great size, are encountered. The formations here are of volcanic materials, while some have a decided sandstone appearance, and farther up the lake are clearly defined exposures of a slaty formation, cut by many quartz veins. The river from here to the canyon has about a three mile current, and occupies a valley of some extent. The banks are low and even marshy in many places, bordered with much good timber, with sloughs filled with duck and muskrat, not to mention the swarms of mosquitos.

CUT BANKS AND MARTINS' NESTS.

A few miles further we come to the first high cut banks which become so general farther down. These are completely honeycombed by martin, that come all this great distance to rear their young. Mile after mile of these banks, furnishing homes for millions of these playful little birds, is passed.

SALMON.

This stretch of the river is the limit of the salmon's travels, few ever reaching Lake Marsh. The mighty waters of the canyon sap the remaining strength after their long journey and it seems strange how this beautiful fish must labor for months against the current, only to die after depositing their spawn. The salmon here are the finest in the world and will average forty pounds each. They run in pairs, the male keeping close to the female, and when the spawn has become ripe enough to be squeezed out by some friendly rock, he is always on hand to cover the whole with a milky substance essential to insure the arrival of the hundreds of little lives which find their way to the mother sea only to return as did their progenitors and furnish food for bruin, for after spawning they soon die.

The bear all come down from their homes in the mountains to dine and fatten on this fish, a part of the head being their favorite morsel. In the month of August dozens of bear can be seen any day along the river.

Many smooth and grassy hills border the river, and a few miles above the canyon Silver creek enters among a confusion of dome-like, sandy hills. The current becomes stronger and the roar of many riffles keeps the canyon constantly in mind. This will be known, however, by a friendly sign on the right hand side reading: "Danger, Stop." The right side should be followed closely here and as soon as the sign is passed a friendly eddy can be easily made just at the entrance of the grand canyon.

GRAND CANYON AND WHITE HORSE RAPIDS.

On the right and at the entrance to the canyon there is a good skidway used by the miners for transporting their boats.

The canyon proper is five-eighths of a mile long, but the distance to portage is nearer one mile, while that run by the boats is three fourths of a mile. The canyon is cut through a horizontal basalt bed and the walls range in height from fifty to one hundred and twenty feet, and are worn into all kinds of fantastic shapes. The canyon has an average width of about one hundred feet and the force of the water of this mighty river, crowded and piled up in this small space, can hardly be realized. The river above has an average width of 250 yards and the water of the canyon must necessarily be deep. I heard of a huge rock just within its entrance, but could see no signs of it either from the walls or from the boat as I passed through. I believe there is little danger in shooting this canyon with a good boat, unless the steersman should lose his head. The water is crowded up to a crest in the center fully four feet higher than at the walls, and little difficulty will be found in keeping the boat on this crest if it is kept under control. But once over the crest there is danger of striking the wall and little would be left of boat or cargo in this case. My boat made the distance of three-quarters of a mile in two minutes and twenty seconds and the experience is surely an exciting one and not to be forgotten.

My boat was strongly built of five-eighth boards, twenty-two feet long and well braced with one and three-quarter inch timbers nailed and clinched with wire nails. It carried about nine hundred pounds of outfit besides ourselves. We removed the camera, plates, a bag of cooked provisions and our guns, stored the rest close and lashed everything tight, covering all with a tarpaulin, thus preventing its filling as it struck its nose through the crest of the heavy combers. When we emerged from the dark walls and entered the eddy on the right at the foot, our boat was leaking badly and nearly every nail was started; this was caused mostly from being overloaded which necessarily made the strain greater. Perhaps an attempted description of this short journey will not be out of place, and while it may satisfy those who never make it, its feebleness will be apparent to those fortunate enough to experience the satisfaction of gazing on this hell of seething waters, after successfully shooting through the dark abyss.

We arranged everything satisfactorily in the boat, tried the steering sweep's strength, discarded all possible clothing even to our heavy boots, took our respective places and pulled far out into the eddy. My partner strained every muscle at the oars to give steerage way that we might enter straight. The ever increasing current caught us and our boat seemed fairly to shoot into the dark shadows of those grotesque and weird walls until it was caught by the recoil of the first great breaker; here it almost stopped and fairly trembled as if in fear to proceed, but only for a moment, then dashed on to its crest and with one mighty bound tried to make the next high place, but it was too heavily loaded and fell far short, shooting through instead, drenching us most throughly. As it raised up the water poured off of the canvas cover and we were rushing on to the next with clouds of spray dashing in blinding sheets against our faces. In the first stretch this was repeated several times until we reached the basin about half way through, which forms an eddy and is comparatively smooth. Here we began to breathe again, having held our breath for just one minute and eight seconds, and prepared for the second and home stretch. This proved to be the worst, as at the last pitch the canyon makes a turn and the force of the water as it strikes the wall and turns back is irresistible, but it is all over so quickly there is no time to turn pale or even to remember just how things were managed. I had my camera on the walls overlooking the canyon and focused it on a high comber and Mr. Bramer was kind enough to work the pneumatic shutter giving instantaneous exposure.

The contrast between those foaming waters and the dark walls of the canyon rendered it a hard object to photograph, but the result can be seen on the opposite page, which will convey some idea of the canyon as seen from the walls above.

The distance of three-fourths of a mile was made in two minutes and twenty seconds, which is the gait of a good trotting horse on a smooth track. Imagine a boat loaded with two men and nine hundred pounds dashing alongside of a light pneumatic sulky drawn by a good trotting horse, and some idea of the trip will be had.

WHITE HORSE RAPIDS.

The White Horse rapids are about two miles below the canyon, and being filled with rapids and sunken boulders this part of the trip should be well looked out before starting. There is one short place where most of the miners portage. The skidway is on the east side and not more than one hundred yards long. By keeping the west bank, little trouble will be found running the whole distance to the head of White Horse, if the boat is under complete control. But if it is unwieldy the portage is preferable. Just before reaching the White Horse there is a comparatively smooth stretch of river giving an opportunity to land on the long point just above the great bend.

The boat can be dropped from here down to the eddy where everything will have to be portaged. The portage here is on the west side. The river is confined between low basalt walls and the last pitch is scarcely ninety feet wide. Here the water presents a formidable spectacle and is seldom run, yet the best boat with good boatmen will, I believe, come through all right. The boats can be lowered by long ropes down to the last pitch where a short portage of a hundred feet will be made. From the entrance of the canyon to the foot of White Horse rapids is about three miles, which can never be made navigable for river steamers.

PROPOSED TRAMWAY ROUTE.

There is to the east a long level valley which runs to the head of White Horse rapids, where a tramway could be easily built and operated; while from the head to the foot of the White Horse a slightly elevated shelf forms a natural roadbed. This occupies the even flow of the volcanic bed and only where the river makes the turn at the head would any work be necessary for the entire length. Power for such a tramway could easily be procured from the falls. The lake boats could connect with this above the canyon, while the river boats could run up to its lower terminus.

Here the country shows great evidence of the glacial period and the low grassy-terraced hills of the east would furnish fine grazing, while to the west they are more abrupt, and further away are fine forests of spruce and pine. Many boats were lost in these three miles of river last spring; some were turned loose and went to pieces on the rocks, while others were swamped in lowering.

An interesting story was told me of two Swedes who came down the river last spring and were carried into the canyon by accident. There were many miners at the portage at the time, and no sooner did the boat strike the rough water, than the Swedes threw up their hands and crouched in the bottom of their boat. It was a good one and rode the waters well until the eddy was reached, when, having no guiding hand, it shot into the eddy instead of passing on down the lower stretch. The current of this eddy is very strong and the walls are about 150 feet high. With all their efforts they could not induce the boat to leave the circle, and they soon gave up the task and lay down in the boat perfectly resigned to their fate. They were entirely out of reach of any assistance from the banks and after about six hours of this circling the boat left the eddy by one of those unaccountable freaks of such places, and they were soon safely landed below.

TAHKEENA RIVER.

This river is a good sized stream. The current is not so swift as that of the Lewis river, which joins about fifteen miles below the White Horse rapids. It is probably little more than half as large as the Lewis river, and is bordered by high hills which to the westward reach the dignity of mountains, apparently of granite. The Tahkeena is said to drain a large lake to the west some seventy miles, and is the inland waterway used in connection with the Chilkat pass, which is made accessible by the west arm of Lynn canal. This pass, while low, is long and less used than formerly by the Indians, and never by the miners. This river has no rapids of any note, making it easy to ascend.

LAKE LABARGE.

Lake Labarge is about twelve miles below the Tahkeena river. These twelve miles of river the most of the distance run through a large valley, much of which is flat and low, scarcely higher than the lake to the east, terminating in the Sandstone range bordering the lake. The river has cut many channels through the bank of sand and clay, and some of these save miles by cutting across. Lake Labarge is about thirty-one miles long, with an average breadth of five miles, and in some places it is much wider. This lake gets very rough and is one of the windiest of the whole system. The formations about this lake are very marked and singular—mostly of limestone to the east—and rise abruptly from the water in some places, while beyond these, still higher mountains rise which separate the Hootalinqua from the waters running into the Lewis. There are many beautiful little lakes in these mountains some five or six hundred feet above the surface of Lake Labarge, which has an elevation of 2100 feet. To the west the hills are wooded more or less. At the southwest end a small stream enters through a broad, level valley, while another enters from the west near its northern end. The outlet here turns to the east and cuts through the hills instead of following the broad, low valley which we had supposed it would follow. The lake lies nearly north and south and seems to be very deep, especially along its eastern shore. After leaving this, the last of the lakes, the current of the river soon increases to five and six miles per hour. The river has cut its way among the jumble of hills leaving it very crooked, many times nearly doubling on itself. The bed is filled with boulders and would probably need some work to make it safe for river steamers. While boats could undoubtedly ascend, it would be impossible to descend with any degree of safety while forced along by the strong current. The hills come down to the water's edge and in some places are well timbered. The cut clay banks are common from here on to the Pelly river.

HOOTALINQUA RIVER.

About twenty-eight miles from Lake Labarge the Hootalinqua river enters from the east and at its confluence with the Lewis seems quite as large. The current is much milder and therefore carries a smaller quantity of water. While this river is known to the miners as the Hootalinqua, Dawson calls it after its Indian name "Teslintoo," Schwatka called it "Newberry," and the original coast survey "Wasathan." This custom of name-changing has been carried on to such an extent that it becomes conflicting, and as the miners are the men who open up the country they are the authority that should be followed. This river has never been explored to any great extent, but it is certain that it is fed by an enormous lake known as Teslin, and this in turn by many rivers of considerable size. This is undoubtedly a fact, as it drains a dry country lying beyond the snow and ice of the Coast range and its volume of water would indicate the extent of country to be considerable. Much flower gold has been found along this river on all the bars, and only the lack of supplies prevents rich discoveries. This will undoubtedly be overcome in the near future, as Captain Healey told me he would establish a trading post there this coming season. The bars for miles below the Hootalinqua have furnished much gold, that of the Cassiar being far the richest. The river has a good five mile current and is bordered by hills of considerable height.

BIG SALMON RIVER.

Thirty-one miles from the Hootalinqua the Big Salmon enters from the same side and is a large river. Little definite information could be obtained concerning this river, except that its bars carry some gold and that its source lies about two hundred miles to the south and east, and like all other rivers of the country flows from a number of lakes. It has been little prospected, but all who have prospected it report gold everywhere. This river, as its name would indicate, is a great salmon stream and many Indians spend the summer months here preparing their winter salmon. The current is mild, compared with the Lewis, and the water much clearer, as are all the waters flowing from the east, while those from the west show signs of glacial action and volcanic deposits. Below the Big Salmon the hills are high and rounded, many wooded to their summits. Some bars have been worked here.

LITTLE SALMON RIVER.

Thirty-five miles farther down, the Little Salmon river enters from the east from among high hills and does not show much valley. This river has never been prospected to any extent and little could be learned of it except as a fishing stream used by the Indians. The river makes many long bends in this distance, fairly doubling on itself. From Little Salmon river to Five Finger rapids the distance by river is fifty-three miles while in a straight line it would scarcely exceed one-half of that distance. The course of the river is very irregular with scarcely any valley.

George McCormack has a small trading post about fifteen miles above Five Fingers, and five and one-half miles farther up he is opening up a vein of coal which shows well a few feet from the surface. It is of a lignite character and burns well.

The banks where cut by the river are of clay, gravel and volcanic matter. They are very high and are constantly sliding into the river. The current from here to the Five Fingers is about five miles per hour. The country is generally well wooded, birch being abundant.

FIVE FINGERS.

This rapid is short, but the drop caused by the five columns of rock, which partly obstruct the river's course, is considerable and would prove an obstruction to river steamers, although it would be possible at a reasonable cost to blast out one of these columns. This could be done in the winter with little difficulty and would widen the channel enough to lessen the fall. Little trouble will be experienced in running this rapid with a good boat, although several accidents have occurred here. The channel to the right is the one usually run. The illustration was taken from the high bank some distance below, from the west side. The country here is generally wooded with terraced, open, grassy slopes on the southern hillsides.

RINK RAPIDS.

These rapids are some six miles below Five Fingers and are formed by a bar of rocks reaching nearly across the river. This, on the west side, is quite as bad as the Five Fingers but on the east there is scarcely a ripple and a small river steamer would have no difficulty in following this shore. In running here, by keeping close to the east shore, it will not be necessary to stop at all. The valley now becomes wider while the hills are less defined. The river rapidly widens also, and islands are numerous. The current runs about five miles an hour while farther down it increases to fully six miles. About thirty miles below some singular formations occur; one particular mound-shaped butte rises out of a flat, while others come down to the river's edge. Some croppings of quartz are seen in these bluffs. Farther down, the river becomes wider and so filled with islands that it is hard to tell where the shores are, until the high hills on the west are reached. These come down to the water very abrupt and the current is increased.

OLD FORT SELKIRK.

Old Fort Selkirk is fifty-five miles from Five Fingers and just below the confluence of the Pelly and Lewis rivers. Here Harper has a trading post and Captain Healey's company winter their boat, the *P. B. Weare.*

On the east side there is a high basalt plateau, said to have come from a large volcano some thirty miles up Pelly river. It has an abrupt front and has crowded the river some distance to the west, which it follows some six or eight miles where it terminates in hills of sand and lime-stone.

Just below the confluence of the Pelly and Lewis rivers is the point at which old Fort Selkirk stood before it was pillaged and burned, August 1, 1852, by the Coast Indians. Only the ruins of the chimneys can now be found. Fine gardens belonging to the mission and post were seen here. A good grazing country of considerable extent surrounds this site. The river from here on for some distance has a uniform width with abrupt hills coming quite down to the water's edge. Farther on the river widens to fully one mile and contains many islands, all well timbered. The formation is mostly limestone with some granite, slate and croppings of quartz everywhere.

WHITE RIVER.

Ninety-six miles from Fort Selkirk the White river enters from the west. It is beyond all doubt the most wonderful of all this great system of rivers. It is a large stream and carries a vast volume of water having an eight to a ten mile current. The water is extremely muddy, due to a white, glassy substance which completely colors the entire Yukon until it is but little clearer than the White river itself. The White discharges its waters into the Yukon with such a force that the roar can be heard for some distance, and this muddy tributary is projected nearly across the swift current of the main river. White river drains a high, mountainous country away to the west, according to the statement of a Tanana Indian, who has traveled the country extensively, and who, with eight others, came from Tanana. They came down White river, to the point on the Yukon where we met them, in a skin canoe built for the purpose. They also informed us that many high mountains and a large lake many days' travel to the west lay near the source of the White, and that one of the mountains was many times higher than the others and was often seen emitting fire and smoke and was known to the Indians as Thunder mountain. I asked them if the mountain was covered with clouds most of the time. They told me that sometimes in summer it could not be seen and that in the winter it was never visible. This would prove that it was not of the Coast range, if such a mountain does really exist.

VOLCANIC ASH DEPOSITS.

The White river must come from a glacial region and probably flows over volcanic deposits, as its sediment is similar to ashes and is noticed all along the river below the lakes. This volcanic ash appears to have been deposited like snow, and is said to cover a vast extent of territory. Dr. Dawson reports finding it all along the Pelly river, but found it of a much greater thickness on the Lewis river at a point directly west of the deposits on the Pelly, thus proving that the seat of action was to the west. That the deposit is of recent date, there can be little doubt, as it overlays driftwood in some of the cut banks of the Lewis and is covered with very little soil. However, all the timber has grown since its fall, as I noticed trees of the largest size growing on drift deposits which overlaid it several feet. Dawson says this ash deposit probably covers 25,000 square miles, and he is undoubtedly the best authority on such matters of any one who has visited that region. His report to the Canadian government shows him to be the closest observer of everything. I do not believe the eruption which deposited this ash took place in the Coast range. I can find no record of its being noticed on the coast or by any of the explorers who visited the vicinity of this range of mountains in this district, or in the Copper river district beyond the Coast range where it should be more evident. This, and the reported burning mountain of the interior, the muddy waters of the White river, the exceedingly muddy condition of all these waters, the fact that the deposit at the time of action was doubtless of a very light character and that the prevailing west winds would prevent its falling to any extent to the west, all these facts go to prove that the action took place near the head waters of the White river, and the possible existence of an active volcano there at the present time.

The Yukon rapidly widens below the White river to fully one

mile and contains many islands, all well timbered. The valley also widens with the river.

STEWART RIVER.

Ten miles below the White river the Stewart river enters from the east and helps swell the already mighty Yukon. The Stewart has a mild current with deep, darkish waters. It is bordered by rolling hills, which in turn are backed by high hills, rising to the dignity of mountains in many places. The bars of the river have furnished lucrative diggings for years to many miners and many hundred miles of tributaries and gulches yet remain to be prospected. It is probably navigable for small river steamers for many miles and is said to drain some large lakes away to the south-east. It is undoubtedly three hundred miles in length, not counting its many tributaries. Just below the mouth on the west are some abrupt hills, apparently of limestone.

SIXTY MILE CREEK.

Seventy miles below the mouth of Stewart river Sixty Mile creek enters from the west. Harper and Ladue have a trading post and a saw-mill here on an island. About one hundred miners annually winter here. Sixty Mile creek has a swift current and is filled with rapids, making it very difficult to ascend. Miller creek enters Sixty Mile creek about seventy miles from its mouth. Little traveling to Miller creek is done all the way by water, for it is much easier to ascend Sixty Mile creek and portage over the Bald hills to the head of Miller. Below Sixty Mile creek the Yukon holds its usual current and contains many islands. The valley is not so broad, however, the hills being abrupt and of various formations, abundant croppings of quartz being seen everywhere.

INDIAN CREEK AND CLONDIKE RIVER.

Thirty miles below Sixty Mile creek, Indian creek enters the Yukon. Here discoveries were made last season that were reported very rich. The stream is rapid, with very little water, and

SIXTY MILE POST

all of peculiar formation, there being no defined range of mountains, but a jumble of bald hills, the glacial drip of which feeds hundreds of tributaries to the larger creeks. The formation of this country will be found marked upon the maps as they occur. These maps cover all of Forty Mile creek and its branches and that part of Sixty Mile creek and its gulches which is being worked to any extent, both the summer and winter trails being marked by dotted lines. The summer trail leads up Forty Mile creek by boat to Moose creek, a distance of twenty-seven miles, then by trail over Bald hills to the head of Miller creek, a distance of thirty-four miles. Poker, Davis, Glacier and Little Gold creeks all lie within a few miles of Miller creek.

MILLER CREEK.

Miller creek thus far has proved to have the richest diggings, various estimates placing the sum taken out last season as high as $300,000. In one claim alone $35,000 were taken out and the place worked was only thirty by one hundred feet, one clean-up being made of 1,100 ounces.

This creek is not more than six miles long with about fifty-four claims, and many of the lower claims are not opened up to any extent as yet. A claim here consists of five hundred feet of the creek and may reach up both sides of the gulch an indefinite distance. The discoverer is allowed two claims or one thousand feet.

Miller creek was prospected and given up three times before it was thought profitable to work, thus showing how difficult prospecting becomes here, owing to the vast quantities of glacial drift everywhere. Miller creek furnishes work for about 125 men, the prevailing pay being ten dollars a day. Provisions and necessities are correspondingly high: potatoes and onions sold for $1 a pound; flour, $19.50 per sack of fifty pounds; gum boots, $18 per pair; butter, $1.50 per pound; whiskey, $1 per glass and other things in proportion. This applies to all mining creeks lying near Miller creek, namely, Davis creek, Pike's gulch, Little Gold creek and Glacier creek. These prices are brought about by the enormous cost of packing from Forty Mile Post to the mines on these creeks.

FREIGHTING.

This is done from Forty Mile Post up to the mouth of Moose creek by freighters of from six to eight tons burden, poled by Indians, and thence over the hills to Miller creek, thirty-four miles farther. Supplies are carried by miners and Indians and even sleigh dogs are used, a good dog carrying as high as fifty pounds. The total distance from Forty Mile Post to the head of Miller creek is about sixty-one miles, and the cost of freighting in summer is $30 per hundred pounds. Two small horses were used here with good result in the summer of '94. The round trip from the mouth of Moose creek to Miller, a distance of thirty-four miles, can be made in three days with a load of 200 pounds. This distance is lessened some by the winter trail. All freighting in winter is done by sleighs with dogs at a cost of $10 to $13 per hundred pounds. They haul much larger loads than one would suppose and make long distances over the ice and snow. Their food consists entirely of dried salmon and they lie down at night in the snow to rest and sleep after their long, hard day's work, often with the thermometer down to sixty degrees below zero.

GLACIER CREEK.

This creek lies east of Miller creek, three miles distant, running nearly parallel with it, and being separated only by a high range of hills. It has been prospected several times but was not located till last season. Some preliminary work has been done towards opening it up. Such claims as were prospected to any great extent promise fair to be equally as rich as those on Miller creek. The excitement occurred in August and was started by some prospectors who discovered rich finds in the old dumps of previous prospectors. Within six hours the whole creek was staked out, the locators being mostly the hired miners of Miller creek.

PROSPECTING AND MINING.

Prospecting in this country is very difficult owing to the character of the surface, the general formation being soft, the hills having been worn smooth by glacial action which left a layer of drift over the whole country to a depth of from five to fifteen feet. This is frozen the whole year with the exception of a few inches on the surface.

The method of prospecting is usually carried on by sinking a number of holes to bed-rock across the bed of the creek, or crosscutting it by a tunnel and testing the dirt every few feet by panning, thus locating the pay-streak. After a creek has been prospected and located then it becomes necessary to remove the glacial drift. The trees and roots are removed and a stream of water turned on which with the help of the sun in time bares the pay-streak. The course of the water is then turned along the side of the hill, a dam built and sluice-boxes erected. These are made with corrugated bottoms which catch and retain the gold. They are given a grade regulated by the coarseness of the gold; that is, if the gold is of an exceedingly fine quality, the grade will be slight, but if of a coarser character, a greater pitch can be given, which is always preferable as the swiftness of the water enables a greater quantity of dirt to be handled. The lack of water in these gulches proves a great hinderance in many cases. The seasons are dry and only the glacial drip of the hills can be depended upon.

A method lately adopted on these creeks by which mining can be done in winter has proved profitable besides doing away with the long period of idleness. This is called *burning*, and is done by drifting, melting away the frost by fire and taking out only the pay dirt, leaving the glacial drift and surface intact. The pay dirt thus removed is easily washed in the spring when water is plenty.

BED-ROCK CREEK.

This creek is about three miles distant from Miller creek to the west and runs nearly parallel with it. Although it has been prospected to some extent, and some claims have been located, it has not proved very satisfactory; yet it may contain gold in paying quantities. The creek, as its name indicates, is not overlaid with the usual amount of glacial drift and therefore would be much more easily worked. It is much better timbered than the surrounding creeks and carries a greater volume of water, being fed by numerous springs among which are several fine soda and other mineral springs. This creek seems to differ in many respects from any of the others and the geologist might find many surprises in its exceedingly interesting and wonderful formation.

BALD HILLS.

From the summit of the Bald hills at the head of these creeks is one of the grandest scenes on this continent. Scores of sparkling streams, like threads of silver, stretch away toward every point of the compass. To the west high mountains tint the horizon with blue; while to the north and east, beyond the mighty Yukon, a spur of the Rocky mountains can be traced for more than a hundred miles, its snow-capped peaks piercing the clouds. To the northwest the high cut banks of Forty Mile creek can be seen, while beyond, the old standard land mark, whose dome can never be mistaken, no matter from what point of view it is seen, looms up grandly.

FORTY MILE POST.

Forty Mile Post is situated on the point of land formed by Forty Mile creek and the Yukon. This point at times of high water is converted into an island, some portions of which are occasionally submerged. Beyond this and bordering the hills is a fine table-land, extensive enough to make a fine townsite. The officers of the Canadian government have made sufficient reserves here for custom buildings and police headquarters. This tract, I believe, is under the immediate direction of Captain C. Constantine.

The town at present consists of ten saloons, McQuestion & Co's store, two blacksmith shops, two restaurants, three billiard halls, two dance houses, opera house, cigar factory, barber shop, two bakeries and several breweries and distilleries. The town has a recorder and the sum of five dollars is charged for the filing and staking of lots. In order to hold a lot the owner must erect a building within a certain time; if it is to be a cabin, it must be built within six months after location.

The buildings are all made of logs chinked with moss; the roofs are of poles covered with a layer of moss with a foot of dirt over all.

Living is reasonable, two dollars a day being charged for board by the two restaurants while cabins can be rented for from thirty to thirty-five dollars for the winter season.

DOGS.

One of the first things to attract attention here, as well as throughout the entire Yukon basin, is the great number of dogs. They are closely related to the wolf, and if they are not natural born thieves they are nothing. They usually celebrate the arrival of all new comers by a general fight. They will steal anything from a pair of boots to a side of bacon; one actually stole a paste pot from me while I was at work on some pictures. They manifest a great degree of cunning in their attempts at stealing.

Snowshoes, dog harness and the like, as well as all kinds of uncanned meats have to be cached. This is done by erecting a strong house upon posts, twelve or fifteen feet above ground, for the safe keeping of all such articles. As previously stated, these dogs are used in freighting to the mines in winter. An additional charge of two cents a pound is made on bacon and all uncanned meats on account of the extra trouble to keep that class of goods from the dogs. The howling of wolves would be pleasant music compared with the howling of these dogs at night. Under the least provocation, in the calm of night, one will start in and almost simultaneously every dog within five miles will join in a general uproar. They often continue their howlings for hours. In spite of all these inconveniences the dog is to the inhabitants of the Yukon, what the reindeer is to the Laplander, the horse to the inhabitants of the plains. In winter they are hitched to a sleigh and in summer loaded with packs. When the day comes for them to be replaced by the reindeer that roam Bald hills in bands of thousands, all will rejoice, for the dogs are always partially loaded with their own food, and in cases of distress furnish poor food even for a famished miner. The flesh of the reindeer is a delicacy and they are able to subsist in all parts of the country.

FORT CAUDHY.

Just below where Forty Mile creek unites with the Yukon, on a beautiful wooded shelf, high above the river, protected from the north and west winds by high hills, rests Fort Caudhy. This town was founded by Captain Healey and is the headquarters of the North American Transportation and Trading Company, better known here as Capt. Healey's Company. While this company is a new-comer, having been there only three years, yet in that time the opposition started by it has reduced the price of living about one-half. This is of the greatest importance to the development of the country and makes it possible to work diggings that were previously abandoned. They have erected large warehouses, a saw-mill, free reading room, billiard hall and many fine cabins. Their boat, the *P. B. Weare*, is a modern river boat and is able to carry a cargo of 350 tons.

COAL CREEK.

The river below Forty Mile creek is bordered on both sides by abrupt hills with no valleys whatever, the islands becoming less numerous. Coal creek enters from the east about seven miles below the mouth of Forty Mile creek. It is quite rapid and navigable for a few miles only. The formation is limestone with frequent croppings of coal. Extensive leads of coal are reported to exist some distance from the river. The coal of this country, as far as known, is lignite in character and seems of recent formation. In fact many parts of the country appear to be undergoing the later processes of the carboniferous period. Coal creek cuts its way back to a high range of mountains, evidently a spur of the Rocky mountains. The river does not cut this range but flows around what appears to be the terminus. The country south and east of the range is well timbered but nothing further is known of it. From the mouth of Coal creek on to the Yukon flats the characteristics of the river remain about the same. The current is strong, the hills abrupt and the formation sand and limestone with conglomerates and shales. Crystalline gneiss and granite veins are not uncommon.

CIRCLE CITY.

About 170 miles from Forty Mile creek, on the west bank, an elevated table-land borders the river. This is just within the Yukon flats. Here the new camp of Circle City was founded in the fall of 1894. It is the distributing point for the vast region of Birch creek and will undoubtedly become the metropolis of the Yukon, not only on account of the extensive auriferous deposits known to exist there, but principally because it is on American soil. More than one hundred men have prospected the creek and the bars adjacent to Birch creek, and all agree that it bids fair to rival the now famous Forty Mile creek. On the opposite page is a view taken of the first supplies landed at that point, September 5, 1894. Two buildings for stores were soon under construction and it is probable that 300 men passed the present winter there. The town is laid off into streets, main street facing the river. It has

First Supplies at Circle City

scarcely supplies enough in the country to carry the number wintering there through, it will be impossible to obtain any to freight to the mines, nor can prospectors obtain supplies for a summer's prospecting trip until the first boats arrive, which will be well into the summer, too late to start on an extensive trip. This will occur again next year, unless the company more than doubles the amount of supplies for that year, as in all probability more than double the number of men will winter there.

PREACHER CREEK.

Preacher creek enters Birch some sixty miles below the portage and is about one hundred and twenty-five miles in length. It has been prospected very little but its head waters are said to cut a country of very peculiar formation. Two men who prospected there last year found little gold but much else of interest. They expect to make a second trip the coming year.

The creek was named after a preacher who made an exploration trip of some length in search of fossils. It is reported he found high clay banks some seventy miles from its mouth. These banks were about three hundred feet high and overlaid a layer of driftwood some two hundred feet down. Much of this driftwood was well preserved and of much larger dimensions than any growth in the country at present, some of the trees being fully four feet in diameter. The creek is constantly undermining its banks, thus bringing down great slides of clay and wood which completely fill the creek at times. This goes to prove beyond a doubt that the great Yukon flats were at one time a vast lake, much larger than any fresh water lake existing to-day.

YUKON FLATS.

The Yukon flats are traversed by the river from Circle City to the Lower Ramparts, a distance of four hundred miles. Their width equals their length. This tract includes the mouth of the Porcupine, Birch and several smaller creeks. At the point the river leaves these flats it cuts its way through a low range of mountains called the Rampart mountains. It then turns to the west and follows the range some three hundred miles farther. This range of mountains was undoubtedly the barrier that formed the great lake of the past. This lake must have been larger than Great Slave lake and quite as deep. There must have been a fall mightier than Niagara at its outlet before the great barrier was worn or broken away. All this time the mighty Yukon and the Porcupine were depositing the wash from hundreds of streams and mountains, forming the flats of to-day. Now this silt is carried down the river and deposited at its mouth forming the delta of the Yukon. Some idea of the enormous amount of sediment annually deposited may be had by noting what takes place along the banks of the main river and numerous tributaries, upon the breaking up of the ice in the spring. Often cakes of solid ice eight feet thick and acres in area come tearing down the river, cutting and plowing the banks until they become so undermined that they scarcely sustain their own weight. Larger fields of ice follow, borne madly along by the irresistible current, and strike the overhanging mass of earth. With a roar like an avalanche the high bank gives way and is precipitated upon the field of ice below, nearly sinking it. Slowly rising, it throws off most of its weight of rocks, gravel and earth. The rocks and gravel sink but the finer particles are kept moving along by this rapid current. A pail of this water allowed to stand over night will contain a half-inch of sediment in the morning. This same current bears these ice-floes onward to be deposited upon some sand bar near the river's mouth, or to be carried far out into Behring sea. Nearly every cake gathers a load on its long journey down, some carrying rocks, others trees, sand or clay, all helping to transform and build up in a manner unsurpassed by any other river in the world. Only such rivers as rise in the south and flow northward, carry such fields of ice in the breaking up; the Yukon's only northern competitors are the Mackenzie and Lena of Siberia.

FOSSILS.

After the waters of this great lake subsided, it became the home of the mastodon which it is believed roamed this vast northern waste in countless numbers and of a size beyond any living thing of the present age. Tusks of fossil ivory are numerous throughout these northern regions besides bones and teeth of a marvelous size. An island known as Mammoth island seems to have been a burying place for one of these herds, remains being piled up in great profusion. The habitat of these animals seemed to range to the westward into the Copper river district and remains are found throughout the Birch creek district and even in the Ratzel mountains. Nearly the whole basin furnishes some fossils, but the flats and country adjacent contain the greatest abundance. Many believe the unexplored country toward the head of Copper river contains living specimens. Many tales are told by Indians from that region of huge woolly beasts with horns like the trunk of the birch tree. They say that in winter puffs of steam issue from their nostrils like that from a steamboat. The stories of their size are interesting even to one acquainted with the Mission Indians. Badlam in his Wonders of Alaska tells of tusks bought by the Alaska Trading Company with flesh and blood still adhearing to them. He has also heard of a huge bear that inhabits the higher mountains of the Yukon country whose legs are longer on one side than on the other, thus facilitating his lonely meanderings on the sides of the cloud-swept peaks. I have no doubt if Badlam had met one of those favored freaks of nature he would have learned a great deal more about them, for it would seem that an animal thus constructed would experience great difficulty in turning and making off in the opposite direction, unless the same providence had constructed it like a double ender, with search-lights at either end.

LOWER RAMPARTS.

The Rampart mountains are followed by the river many miles after leaving the flats, and no streams of any note enter until the Tanana river is reached. This river is probably six or seven hundred miles long with many tributaries. It drains that country lying between the Copper river and the Yukon as far south as the White river. This river is little known and the Indians there are reported hostile. The country about the head waters will undoubtedly prove one of the richest gold fields of the whole country and prospectors will probably push their way there within the next two years.

NUKLUKYETO.

Nuklukyeto is situated on the north bank just below the mouth of the Tozikakat river. The Alaska Commercial Company has a post here, run by Al. Meyhue who has been in the country for more than thirty years. The trade here is almost entirely with the Indians, many of the Tanana Indians coming all the way from the head waters of the Tanana in summer to trade.

KOYUKUK RIVER.

This river enters from the north and is the first large river after leaving the Tanana. It enters the Yukon about five hundred miles below that river and is navigable for many miles. It is quite as large as the Tanana but has a much milder current. The Alaska Commercial Company has a small steamer that supplies their posts on this river as well as the missions. Gold has been found on this river in paying quantities. Nulato, a trading post of the Alaska Commercial Company, is situated on the same side of the river some distance below. From here on the river is much wider, yet losing little of its force of current. The country presents a sameness on this lower river that becomes monotonous even on the down trip, with the boat making as high as twenty-two miles an hour. It must seem much more monotonous on the up trip on account of the slow progress of the boat.

LOWER RIVER NATIVES.

Indians of an inferior class become more numerous as the mouth is approached. Their fishing camps are passed at almost every turn of the river and they have fish-traps at every eddy and protected place. A large number died last winter owing to the severe cold, floods and lack of food. Their food consists almost entirely of fish, and the only clothing worn by many is made from prepared salmon skins. Boots and gloves are also made from salmon skins. These Indians are lazy and it is with difficulty that they can be induced to cut wood for the steamers. There are very few fur-bearing animals in this section of the country, hence wood is about the only means of barter they have. It is very abundant along the banks of the river.

The Innoko and Anvik rivers are the only other streams of any importance that enter the Yukon from here on. After passing those rivers the current becomes much milder and the river wider. Islands are passed near the mouth, some of which have a total length of one hundred miles. The flats and sand bars make feeding and hatching ground for thousands of wild geese. The mouth of the river spreads out to a great width and its numerous channels are filled with sand bars. Probably hundreds of miles of this low land has been filled in with the silt brought down by the swift current of this mighty volume of water. Bering sea for miles is shoaled to such an extent that vessels drawing more than a few feet of water have to land their cargos at St. Michael's island, about sixty miles from the mouth of the river, and the river boats are compelled to make this stretch of open water.

SAINT MICHAEL'S ISLAND.

Here the trading companies of the Yukon district have their principal warehouses. The Alaska Commercial Company has been established here for years and has fine painted buildings presenting a pleasing appearance. A new company, **The North American Trading and Transportation Company**, is also building fine large warehouses and as it is a wideawake, progressive company, it will undoubtedly have as fine buildings as the other has. They both carry a large stock of goods through the winter and many men could find comfortable quarters here, if by accident supplies run short up the river, which is liable to be the case if a very great number of men go into the mines this spring.

The ice does not leave the mouth of the river and about Saint Michael's until the first of June. Ships loaded for this island seldom find it convenient to land their cargo before June 20. This makes the running season for the river boats little more than three months. In that time they can usually make three trips to Forty Mile Post, extending one trip up as far as the Pelly, if no accident happens to delay them. Accidents are always possible owing to the constant changing of the sand bars. To run a boat upon one of those bars means much delay especially if it occurs on the down trip. These river boats will connect at Saint Michael's with steamers running to Seattle and San Francisco. A time-card can be found on another page, giving the necessary information concerning the time of leaving points along the route. These boats connect with the mail boat for Sitka and way points. The trip along the coast is one of great interest. Many noted points are passed and active volcanoes seen. Wild fowl, fur seal, walrus and whale can be seen from the ship's deck almost any day. The curio seeker can reap a rich harvest, for few who visit this country have time or inclination to indulge in the collection of specimens. The Indians about Saint Michael's are very ingenious and industrious. A collection there would consist chiefly of ivory fashioned into everything from a symbolic representation of the history of the family to an expected addition.

NAVIGATION ON THE YUKON.

The navigable waters of the Yukon and its tributaries are almost unlimited. The Lewis can undoubtedly be ascended to the foot of White Horse in a suitable boat, while the lakes above would furnish hundreds of miles of navigable waters. The Pelly could also be ascended a good distance, while many of its branches are also navigable. The Stewart, Tahkeena, Hootalinqua and its lake connections, would make fine water ways; while the Porcupine, Tanana, Koyukuk, Anvik and White rivers, Birch creek, Salmon river and many others, to the extent of many thousand miles will in time be navigated by steamers. At present there are two large boats running from St. Michaels to Pelly river. One, the *Arctic*, owned by the Alaska Commercial Company, is used to supply their stations at Forty Mile Post, Sixty Mile and Pelly rivers. This company has done a trading business for many years and has large warehouses at St. Michael's, sixty miles from the mouth of the river. They also run several smaller boats to their stations along the lower river and will undoubtedly add a new and larger boat to their fleet in the spring. The *P. B. Weare*, I am informed, is the largest boat navigating these waters at present. It is owned by the North American Trading and Transportation Company and is used to supply their stations along the river. It is a large, modern river boat with large double boilers and consumes about twenty-five cords of wood per day. The two companies will double the amount of supplies this year and will undoubtedly be able to supply all who visit the mines the coming season. Connections will be made at St. Michaels with boats for San Francisco and Sound points. The following passenger rates are now charged: From Forty Mile Post to St. Michaels, first-class, $50.00, second-class, $30.00; to San Francisco, first-class, $175.00, second-class, $150.00. The North American Trading and Transportation Company will run passenger steamers from San Francisco and Seattle. The boats will accommodate about one hundred passengers. Tourists, miners and others wishing to go to the Yukon country without the hardships accompanying the trip down the river and at a reasonable price will patronize the North American Trading and Transportation Company's boats.

TAKU ROUTE.

The Canadian government is making a preliminary survey of this route and will build a trail within the year, if such concessions as are necessary can be had from our government. This trail would open up all their extensive country lying beyond the Coast range down to the 141st meridian, most of which is a good grazing country as well as being rich in minerals. This route leads up the Taku Inlet to the Coast range, thence by a low pass a distance of about eighty-five miles to waters running into Lake Teslin. The pass is said to be timbered the entire distance and to run through a fine grazing country. By striking the waters of Teslin lake, thence across this lake and down the Hootalinqua, no falls are encountered other than the Five Fingers which offer no great obstacles. This would always prove an easy route but would, in case of a trail by way of Chilkoot or White pass, be used only for the country not reached by those trails, they being so much shorter than the Taku.

Should our government grant such concessions as the Canadian government will ask for, such a trail would prove the greatest detriment to our interests on the Pacific coast. Not only the wholesale houses on the Sound but the outfitting establishments of Juneau would suffer thereby. Victoria would at once come into prominence and English goods would take the place of American goods. Not only would this hold true in their own territory, but large quantities of those goods would find their way across the line and supply miners on our side of the present imaginary boundary. When the boundary is definitely established, it will be difficult to enforce custom regulations. If our government is not willing to assist in the development of Alaska, it should see to it that what has been accomplished by private enterprise shall not be injured by foreign competition.

WHITE PASS.

This is undoubtedly the best pass, all things considered, that cuts the Coast range. It is at least one thousand feet lower than the Chilkoot and little higher than the Taku. It is reported timbered the entire length. Its salt water terminus is about eighty-five miles north of Juneau and ocean steamers can run up to the landing at all times, where there is a good townsite, well protected from storms. The pass lies through a box canyon surrounded by high granite peaks and is comparatively easy. The first seven miles from salt water lie up the bottom lands of the Shkagway river through heavy timber. Then for about seven miles farther the way is over piles of boulders and moraines which would prove the most expensive part of the trail. This trail would not exceed thirty-two miles in length and would strike Windy arm of Tagish lake or Taku arm coming in farther up the lake. All of this part of the lake is well timbered and accessible to Lake Bennett and its connections. White pass could be used as a mail route any month in the year.

CHILKOOT PASS.

This pass is the shortest of all the passes but the highest by at least one thousand feet. It is the one always used by the miners and is the route followed in the pages of this guide. It starts at the head of Taiya inlet and follows the bottom lands of the Taiya river for some eight miles, where it enters the canyon. The Sheep camp is at timber line and from there the scene is one of extreme desolation, occupied only by glaciers and mountain sheep. No vegetation of any kind can be seen for miles around the summit. Healey & Wilson have a trading post and outfitting establishment at Taiya. They will give all necessary assistance in securing packers over this trail. The total length of this trail from Wilson's to Lake Lindeman is about twenty-four miles, although a second short portage at the foot of Lindeman will have to be made. If this trail should ever become the improved route, this piece of river could be made navigable for lighters.

CHILKAT PASS.

The Chilkat trail leads over the Chilkat pass and is about one hundred and twenty-five miles in length from the head of Chilkat inlet to where it strikes the waters of Tahkeena river. This was the old trail used by the Indians to and from the interior and leads all the way through to Old Fort Selkirk by land. Jack Daulton has used this trail at times in taking horses to the interior, portaging to the Tahkeena, then by raft down that river to the Lewis, thus proving that the Tahkeena is navigable for a small sternwheel steamer for a distance of some seventy miles.

POSSIBLE RAILROAD ROUTE.

As the mines of the Yukon are developed and the basin becomes populated with the large number that must necessarily follow within a few years, means of quicker mail and transportation facilities will be needed. When the Siberian & Arctic railroad shall become a reality trains could leave Chicago by way of Winnipeg and reach the Yukon basin in three days' run; thence on to Behrings straits, which could easily be tunnelled. Four days out from Chicago would land one on Siberian soil. This would open up the greatest commercial route the world has ever known. Three thousand miles of this route are already built and operated by the Russian government, and with the more liberal views of that government, which seem to be assured in the near future, and the constant concentration of capital which is seeking great enterprises, a populated country through which to run, and the comparatively few obstacles in the construction of such a road, all go to assure its success. At no far distant day this railroad could run parallel with the Rocky mountains and follow the high table-land all the way to the Yukon without encountering any obstacles whatever in an engineering sense, and the whole distance to the straits would prove no more difficult than building a road across our plain-country. This route would soon become the tourist route to all Europe. No longer would the dangers of the sea and the ever-dreaded seasickness be considered in a contemplated trip abroad.

RESOURCES.—COPPER.

Copper will undoubtedly prove in the near future one of this country's greatest resources. Ever since Alaska was discovered the Indians have shown much native copper, and mountains of this ore are said to exist in the Copper river region. This region is so little known, however, that much time must elapse before it will become accessible. The deposits on the Yukon and its tributaries must soon draw capital in their direction.

IRON AND COAL.

Vast beds of iron and coal are known to exist in many parts of Alaska. Especially is this true of the Yukon, and when the various modes of travel shall demand cheap fuel, then another of the Yukon's resources will come to the front.

PLATINUM.

Platinum is found in nearly all the Yukon country in association with gold, and it may some day prove a rich field for this metal.

GAME—MOOSE.

That the Yukon basin is a fine game country, all who have visited it admit. The upper country abounds in moose, bear, caribou and much smaller game. White river is reported by the Indians to be a great moose country, the moose there growing to a greater size than in any other part of the American continent. When fat its flesh is always tender and palatable. This is probably due to the rapid growth and tenderness of all vegetation. In summer some of the moose of that region have a wonderful spread of horns and reach a weight of 1,500 pounds. It is one of the principal sources of food for the Indians who find little trouble in killing them at all seasons of the year. The moose, owing to its great size and strength, can procure food despite the deep snows and severe cold. They are not dainty, and will eat almost anything, so that they are fat even in early spring. The skins are coarse and brown when tanned, and are used by the Indians for gloves, moccasins and clothing and even for their lodges. The moose, unlike other ruminants, is a fighter and the femal, single-handed, will protect her young from a whole pack of wolves, and the bull in the fall is an ugly customer even for the hunter to tackle.

CARIBOU.

The woodland caribou is found throughout the lake and upper river country. It averages nearly twice the size of the barren land caribou or reindeer and its habits are also quite different. It never migrates toward the north in summer, but travels directly the opposite way. The caribou here have great powers of endurance and can trot at a gait equal to that of the best horse. In deep snow it is almost useless to pursue them, their wide flat hoofs and the manner in which they spread them, enabling them to keep quite on top of the snow. They are much more strongly built than the barren land caribou and the horns are much stronger and rounder. This species is almost untamable and shows no inclination to work like their cousins in the Bald hills.

BARREN LAND CARIBOU OR ARCTIC REINDEER.

This animal, altogether different from the woodland caribou, occupies the Bald hills near the Arctic circle where food is so scarce that it is constantly on the move, having to migrate to the south in winter. In the severest winters its range is many hundred miles in that direction. While it and the woodland caribou were originally of one species, its mode of living differs so widely from its cousin that its habits and appearance have changed until it can no longer be considered a very near relative to the noble monarch of the woods, that leads a life of perfect idleness and plenty in the rich pine-clad lands to the south. It is not to be wondered that with their decrease in size their manner and temper have also changed and that, with a little coaxing, they readily become beasts of burden. When the time comes for the dogs to give way to their more favored successors everybody in this great country will rejoice. The past five winters about Forty Mile creek have been unusually severe and great herds have ranged further south than usual. It is estimated that no less than five thousand were killed last year in this vicinity. The herds are reported to number hundreds of thousands. Their horns which are counted by the hundreds on the Bald hills, are more slender and have a much greater spread than the woodland caribou, thus causing them little difficulty in ranging the sparcely wooded country. All are provided with the snow shovel reaching quite down to the point of the nose, to assist them in procuring the reindeer moss and lichens in the country they inhabit. This is undoubtedly the reason why the female as well as the male is provided with antlers. The endurance of these animals, if not over estimated, is wonderful and the ease with which they make long journeys through deep snow or over the soggy moss of this country would well fit them for the sleigh or freighter.

BEAR.

There are many species of bear in Alaska and probably the St. Elias grizzly attains a greater size than any other bear in the world. If he is not a fighter he is surely not a coward. This bear is found in the St. Elias Alps and many of the ranges of Alaska, but is more common in the high ranges of mountains east of the Yukon river, below Sixty Mile creek. On the Clondike river they are so numerous as to prevent the Indians from hunting there when fish are plenty. This bear, like the whole bear family, is a great fish eater. It is during the fish season only that this bear leaves its haunts in the high mountains for the lowlands. It likes variety and is more of a meat eater than its less dignified brother, the common or brown bear. Several men who have come in contact with this bear remember it to the extent of a leg or arm and even think themselves lucky to escape with their lives. Some of the skins of this bear are enormous in size and one skull I examined was beyond comparison with anything in the bear line I have ever seen. This St. Elias grizzly when young looks almost white at a distance. It stands higher than other bear and is wary even in this remote region beyond any animal I have ever hunted. On the other hand the brown and the black bear of this region are easily approached and especially when nosing along the banks of streams searching for food. In one case we actually run our boat within thirty feet of one on a clear morning while our portable stove was yet burning having cooked breakfast in the boat.

MOUNTAIN GOAT.

This animal, while probably smaller than the Rocky mountain goat further south, is identical. Its weight will average perhaps one hundred pounds and both sexes have horns. Its home is on the cloud-swept peaks surrounded by nature's solitudes and it seems most content in its gloomy surroundings, when the thunderbolt goes crashing down the rugged sides of the canyon or where the steeps are swept by the mighty avalanche. Its coat is well adapted to its rugged home. Under the long outer hair a fleecy wool protects it in its wonderful leaps from rock to rock. Its legs are straight and stiff and its horns are black. The pelt makes fine robes and is much prized by the Indians.

MOUNTAIN SHEEP.

This animal is found throughout Alaska, being more numerous in the Coast range of mountains than in the interior. It attains a much larger size than the goat, and a ram may often be found weighing three hundred pounds. It is among the wariest of all hoofed game of the American continent. They are hardly worth the time and trouble that are usually consumed in securing them. Its coat is of light gray color and some hunters claim a great delicacy for its flesh.

LYNX.

The North American lynx is abundant throughout the upper river and lake country. It probably attains a larger size there than in any other part of the continent. It is easily trapped and any rifle kills it readily. Although large and strong its tenacity of life is far below all other species of the cat family. The pelt is finely furred and makes excellent robes. Its principal food is the rabbit which abounds throughout that country. Its legs and feet are large and powerful and well covered with hair, giving it rather a clumsy appearance which is turned to one of ludicrousness when frightened. At such times the short, stubbed tail stands erect, the back is arched, and with whiskers standing straight out it makes off by a succession of spasmodic jumps in a way that often totally disconcerts even the old hunter.

WOLVES.

Alaska, like all of North America, is more or less inhabited by wolves. The gray timber wolf of average size is found there. It is so wary as to be seldom seen by man. It has all the cunning of the fox and like all varieties is a coward, except when found in great numbers. In the interior they are numerous. In parts of the Coast country they exist in such numbers that no deer are found on the main land along the whole coast, although the islands are exceedingly well stocked with them.

WOLVERINE.

This animal is probably more plentiful throughout the upper river and lake sections than in any other part of the world. Its peculiar habits and singular appearance are little known even to most naturalists. I cannot recall ever having seen it in captivity. The body is heavy and covered with long hair and fur much prized by the Indians as trimming for their winter garments. Its legs, although short, do not prevent it from making long journeys through deep snow. As there is scarcely any limit to its food capacity, it is continually on the move, yet so wary and careful that it is seldom seen.

FISH.

While the salmon is by far the most important fish of the Yukon there are many varieties of fine fish, the ever cold water keeping their flesh hard and palatable at all seasons of the year. Probably next to the salmon in importance comes the white fish, of which there are several varieties, some reaching a good size. They are found throughout almost the entire river basin.

Lake trout of a good size are found everywhere in the lake country. A species of fish, known to the miners as lake cod, is also found in the lakes. It seems to be a cross between the salmon and white fish, having characteristics of each. It is of good size and rises readily to a troll. Throughout the summer months landlocked salmon, similar to those of Maine and Canada, abound in the lakes. Grayling or arctic trout is found in the rivers. It rises readily to a fly, the small black being the best. A small piece of black thread fastened around the hook will answer the purpose. They frequent the mouths of small streams and falls and are found in great numbers about the canyons and White Horse rapids. Pike are numerous about the lower river, while the sucker is found everywhere. Miners provided with gill nets need have no fear of starving. Along the river anywhere in the summer and fall by such means they could readily lay in a supply sufficient to last throughout the winter.

DISCOVERY OF GOLD IN THE YUKON BASIN.

There seems to be no definite authority as to when and where gold was first discovered in the Yukon basin. No two miners agree on this subject. Gold is reported to have been found by the Hudson Bay Company's men early in the sixties. George Holt is credited by Dawson as probably the first white man to cross the Coast range for the purpose of prospecting. The date of Holt's journey is given as 1878 and whether he followed the trail over the Chilkoot or White pass is not certain. He descended the lakes to Lake Marsh then followed the Indian trail to the Hootalinqua, returning by the same route in the fall. The *Coast Pilot* gives the date of Holt's journey as 1872 or 1874. On his return he reported having found coarse gold near or on the Hootalinqua river and while no coarse gold has since been found in that locality the bars of that river have yielded much flour gold. This lends some color to Holt's story which may yet be confirmed. In 1880 a prospecting party was organized at Sitka under the leadership of Edward Bean. They established friendly relations with the Chilkats and Chilkoots and were permitted to cross the range by way of Chilkoot pass to Lake Lindeman, where they built boats and descended the Lewis as far as the Hootalinqua. The party numbered about twenty-five, one of whom informed Dawson that gold was found in a small stream fifteen miles above the canyon the diggings yielding $2.50 per day. The same year Slim Jim, now residing at Juneau, and John Mackenzie crossed the Chilkoot pass and probably other parties followed within the year. According to the *Coast Pilot* a party of four miners crossed the range in 1881 and descended the Lewis as far as Big Salmon river, which they ascended for some 200 miles, finding gold on all of its bars some of which paid well. This find may be characterized as the first gold discovered in paying quantities in the Yukon basin.

In 1884 and 1885 some mining was done on the Pelly and Hootalinqua rivers. Some miners reached the Stewart in the spring of 1886 and Cassiar bar was also located the same year and actively worked during the season. This was the richest bar ever located on the Yukon or any of its tributaries yielding many thousands of dollars. Late in the autumn of the same year coarse gold was discovered on Forty Mile creek. The announcement of this discovery drew off all the miners from the upper river country. In 1887 a miner named Williams perished on the summit of Chilkoot pass in trying to bring out the news. The bars of Forty Mile creek were worked for a few years at good profit, but since the discovery of coarse gold in the gulches they have been abandoned. It may be truly said that mining in this country is only begun and that only a few of the most accessible streams have even been prospected. All the larger rivers of the upper country furnish flour gold which increases in coarseness as the rivers are ascended. Thus it is clear that the surrounding gulches in many places must furnish exceedingly rich diggings. The territory cut by these streams is almost unlimited. One hundred thousand men could prospect the Yukon basin and be lost to one another. The greatest drawback is the limit of supplies. This will be overcome in the near future as the companies there at present are wideawake to the needs and possibilities of the country. I can see only a bright future for the entire Yukon basin as a mining country, not only in the auriferous deposits but in the vast leads of quartz found throughout the entire region.

SOURCE OF THE YUKON.

Much controversy from time to time has been indulged in as to the true source of the Yukon, and as to its name. The name Pelly was given to the whole river down to the Porcupine by early explorers, while the name Yukon was first applied in 1846 by Mr. J. Bell of the Hudson Bay Company. He reached the main river by descending the Porcupine from the Mackinzie, and called it by its Indian name. R. Campbell, an officer of the Hudson Bay Company, also descended the Pelly as far as the Porcupine, and named the Lewis, Stewart and White rivers. But not until the publishing of the Coast survey map of 1869 did the river become generally known as the Yukon as far up as the Pelly. Schwatka, who afterwards made an official exploration of the river, changed every name never offering the pretext of an excuse. Thus the nomenclature of the Yukon and its tributaries became further confused. Schwatka applied the name Yukon to the Lewis, giving Lake Lindeman as its true source. There was some justification for this inasmuch as the Lewis carries the greater volume of water. Lake Lindeman and its connections, it would seem, are much smaller and shorter than the Toko Arm and its connections. Thus while the Lewis carries the larger volume of water, it is far shorter and drains a smaller country than either the Hootalinqua or the Pelly. The Lewis, draining as it does the Coast range with its perpetual snow and glaciers, maintains its volume of water long after the Hootalinqua and Pelly have reached their lowest summer level. Yet the Pelly is by far the longer river and enough is known of the Hootalinqua to prove it much longer than the Lewis. Those rivers drain a comparatively dry country, the snowfall being light and the rainfall even lighter, therefore the true source of the Yukon yet remains to be definitely settled.

CLIMATE.

The climate in the lake region and down to old Fort Yukon is, although cold in winter and warm in summer, very agreeable. The snow in the upper river country never exceeds three or four feet, often hardly two. In summer little rain falls except during an occasional thunder storm. The summer season is truly one long dream of sunshine, due to the protection of the high Coast range which precipitates the ever present humidity of the coast, leaving the interior dry. The general direction of the winds is inland in summer and directly opposite in winter. This is caused by the rising of the hot air of the interior in summer and in winter by the existence of a persistent north wind which easily forces the coast breezes seaward. The winters, while cold, are so devoid of humidity that the cold is easily endured and one suffers less when the thermometer registers forty below than on the coast at zero.

WINTER CLOTHES.

Most of the miners adopt the native custom of dress to a certain extent. The boots are of several varieties, most of which are made by the Coast Indians. The water boot is made of seal and walrus skins, while the dry weather or winter boot is made in an endless variety of styles, some having fur-trimmed legs elaborately designed, giving them a pleasing appearance. They wear well and range in price from two to five dollars per pair. Trousers are often made of Siberian fawn skin and the skin of the marmot or ground squirrel. The upper garment, called a *parka*, is usually made of marmot skins and trimmed with wolverine around the hood and lower edge, the long hair taken from the sides of the wolverine being used for the hood. This hair is sometimes five or six inches in length thereby protecting the face of the person wearing the hood. Wolverine skins are prized very highly on the coast of Behring sea, and as that animal does not inhabit the coast, the skins are bought by the traders in the lake country and sold to the inhabitants of the coast. In some instances they are bought in San Francisco and taken up to this fur-bearing country for trade. The women's *parka* differs slightly from that worn by the men, being cut up at the sides some ten inches and rounded at the bottom like a shirt. Some of these come all the way from Siberia and are works of art. Some are made of fawn skins and trimmed with the fur of the white wolf. The inside is beautifully embroidered with colored silks and ornamented with otter's fur and dyed feathers. Some of these *parkas* cost as high a one hundred dollars. Good warm flannels can be worn under these and the whole outfit will weigh less than the ordinary clothes worn in a country where the weather gets down to zero. They have an attractive and unique appearance and are rather enjoyed after once worn. They are almost cold proof. For bedding the best blankets to be obtained are used ; also fur robes, those made of lynxs' skins being about the best considering price and wear. A good lynx robe sells for one hundred dollars. Bear, mink and red fox robes are also used. The arctic hare makes cheap and nice robes as well as socks to be worn with the skin boots.

NEW DISCOVERY AT COOK INLET.

Cook Inlet has been prospected for many years but with little success although flour gold is found all along the coast. This washes in with a fine magnetic sand and although worked for some time in the short summer only small wages have been made. One surface claim, after running a ditch some distance for water, was worked with some success. This was on the east coast of the inlet. Another claim located on the Turnagain Arm has been worked for some time with better results, as high as ten dollars per day being made. This attracted some attention and in the spring of 1894 twenty men went to that locality. New diggings were located that, according to report, are quite rich, as high as twenty dollars per day being made. The gold is of a course character and is located over the ridge from Turnagain Arm on the small creek that enters near its mouth. Bed-rock lies near the surface and the creeks are said to have a good grade. Nuggets weighing upwards of one ounce were found and the men from whom I learned the above seemed very sanguine over the prospects and expected to return this spring with provisions for a long stay. To test them I tried to imbue them with the Yukon excitement by telling them of the numerous new and rich finds in that country, but they would not think of leaving their prospects.

THE YUKON RIVER.

What the Amazon is to South America, the Mississippi to the central portion of the United States, the Yukon is to Alaska. It is a great inland highway, which makes it possible for the explorer to penetrate that unknown country where heat and cold for ages have contended for the mastery, to reveal to the world the treasures so long held secret in that ice-vaulted region. A wonderful story will be unfolded as the mysteries are brought to light; but the revelation of the wonders therein contained will of necessity be made very slowly for the reason that the only key to this frozen, rock-ribbed region is carried by the king of day in his triumphant march through the skies and he permits the use of it for only a brief period during the summer of eight to ten weeks. But were it not for this great artery, the Yukon river, which goes pulsating for 2,600 miles through the northwest, bidding defiance to the Frost King with his rivers of ice and mountains of snow, the world would remain in ignorance of the untold wealth of the interior of Alaska.

The Yukon has its source in the Rocky mountains of British Columbia and the Coast Range mountains in southeastern Alaska, about 125 miles from the city of Juneau. This branch of the Yukon, which is known as the Lewis river for 357 miles, the writer has fully explored and a description of the same is given in the preceding pages of this book. The branch that heads in British Columbia is known as the Pelly river and is 600 miles in length. These two branches unite and are then known as the *Yukon*. At the confluence of the Lewis and Pelly rivers is located Fort Selkirk. The Yukon proper is 2044 miles in length and is navigable the entire distance for flat bottom boats with a carrying capacity of from four to five hundred tons. From Fort Selkirk the Yukon flows northwest 400 miles touching the Arctic circle; thence southwest for a distance of 1,600 miles where it empties into Behring Sea. It drains more than 600,000 square miles of territory and discharges one-third more water into Behring Sea than does the Mississippi into the Gulf of Mexico. It is sixty miles wide at its mouth and very shallow which prevents its navigation by seagoing vessels. 1,500 miles inland the river widens out from one to ten miles and a thousand islands send the channel in as many different directions and only natives who are thoroughly familiar with the river are entrusted to pilot boats up the stream during the season of low water.

Unlike the Amazon or Mississippi, with their borders of lowlands, receding hills and flat swampy districts, the Yukon has sawed mountain chains vertically in twain and forced its way through granite walls which have been chiseled into all sorts of fantastic forms by the glaciers of long ago. An unending panorama of grandeur greets the eye of the traveler in the months of June, July and August, as he is borne along on the current of this mighty stream which is only second in size to the largest river of the world. Its banks are fringed with flowers, carpeted with the all-prevailing moss or tundra; birds innumerable sing out a welcome from every tree top, and pitch your tent where you will in midsummer a bed of roses, a clump of poppies and a bunch of bluebells will adorn your camping place. One realizes that he is in a land of paradoxes. He will see a giant glacier sleeping on top the mountain wall along beside which he will see in bloom flowers of almost endless variety. About September 25th the scene of beauty is suddenly changed, when the Winter King advances, sending the alcoholic column eighty degrees below zero, the birds to the south-land, the white man to his cabin, the Indian to his hut and the bear to his sleeping-chamber in the monntains. Every stream becomes a river of ice, every hill a mountain of snow and the valleys of beautiful flowers are changed into a scene of eternal whiteness.

INDIANS ALONG THE YUKON.

In making a journey into the interior of Alaska and down the Yukon river, one comes in contact with ten different tribes, or remanents of tribes, of Indians. The Chilkats who live in the country immediately surrounding Lynn Canal are the largest and most powerful tribe of all. They number only 1000 and are diminishing rapidly every year because of the civilizing (?) influence of strong drink and its attendant vices which the whites have introduced among them. They are avaricious, shrewd and tricky, always a match for the white trader in driving a bargain. They will subject themselves to the most excruciating labor and hardships for days and weeks for a few dollars in silver. They will make long journeys across the mountains into the interior, with heavy loads upon their backs, climb the mountain steeps, struggle across great glaciers, wade icy streams, and, in a thinly clad, half-starved condition, endure privations from which, to the tourist it would seem death would be a welcome relief.

All the tribes of the upper Yukon bear a close resemblance to each other in form and features, which are not unlike the *Siwash* Indian of Puget Sound. The "Sticks" are probably the most stalwart of any. They lay claim to the distinction of being "all same as Boston man." I thought however that I could see some slight chance for improvement, but not being a resident of the Hub I had no quarrel with them on that score.

Until recent years the natives of the Yukon have had to depend entirely upon game and fish for food and for this reason many of the tribes have no permanent abiding place but follow the game from one section of the country to another. They are good hunters and show great skill in the management of their birch bark canoes in the swift waters and rapids of the mountain streams. All the Indians of the upper river dress in the garb of civilization. Traders bring large quantities of food and clothing up the river, thus affording an opportunity for the natives to exchange their furs and dried fish for the necessaries of life, which, to and average Indian, mean plenty of tobacco, a little fire-water, a gun and ammunition. There are three or four missions along the river and as a rule the missionaries are well received. Rev. Mr. and Mrs. Bumpus have had charge of the mission at Forty Mile Post for the past three years. There are 200 communicants at this place who attend all the services of the sanctuary as religiously and regalarly as they light their pipes after a hearty repast on moose meat and dried fish.

The Indians make themselves useful in many ways about the trading posts,—sawing lumber, building log cabins, unloading steamers, acting as guides to miners while crossing the country, packing provisions into the miners during the summer and hauling supplies on dog sledges during the winter.

Further down the river the Indians are not so thrifty. Their principal diet is fish, seal oil and berries. Their hovels are about ten feet square on the ground and have a slanting roof. About four feet above the ground poles are placed across serving as joists. The space above the poles is utilized for storing away dried fish, game, seal skins filled with berries preserved in oil, which are a great luxury among the natives. The space below the poles, which is only high enough for the inmates to sit tailor-like fashion with head and shoulders bent forward, is used for cooking, eating, sleeping, cleaning fish and game of all sorts. They are devoid of all sense of cleanliness and take no sanitary percaution whatever to ward off disease. In one village where we stopped to take on wood we found the dead bodies of three men almost entirely exposed with scarcely any dirt upon them excepting that which they had accumulated during their natural lifetime in the absence of applied soap and water. A more filthy, degraded, loathsome set of creatures it would be hard to find.

The mortality of these tribes is very great and within a few short years they will be creatures of the past and their graveyards will furnish an interesting field for relic hunters, and their bones along with those of the mammoth, giant buffalo, and ichthyosaurus, will adorn the museums of the world while their spirits continue the chase in the "happy hunting ground" beyond.

PURCHASE OF ALASKA.

This little volume upon Alaska would be incomplete without a summary of the history of its purchase and a statement of its area and extent.

Czar Nicholas offered to give Russian America to the United States in 1844 and 45, during Polk's administration, provided our government would pay the cost of transfer and maintain the boundary line at 45° 40'. In 1854 it was offered to the United States and again in 1859, when $5,000,000 were refused. It seemed to be the desire of the Czar to place it beyond the power of England's acquiring it in case of war with that country. During the war of the Rebellion, our government greatly appreciated the moral support given us by the Czar of Russia in sending fleets to the harbors of San Francisco and New York at a time when France and England were on the point of recognizing the government of the Confederate States. Hearing of the desire of the Czar to sell his possessions in America, and appreciating their great value, Secretary of State Wm. H. Seward felt that its purchase would serve a double purpose: it would please the Czar and secure to the United States a valuable territory. Accordingly negotiations were opened in February, 1867. A treaty of purchase was sent to the senate March 30, 1867, reported April 9, ratified May 28, and proclaimed by the president June 20 of the same year. Charles Sumner suggested *Alaska*, the name given to Captain Cook by the natives. The price paid was $7,200,000, less than half a cent an acre. It has proved a profitable investment from the date of purchase, yielding a net profit of 8 per cent. for the first five years upon the price paid. The Salmon industry yielded $7,500,000 in the six years from 1884 to 1890. The Treadwell mine alone has added more than the purchase price to the wealth of the world.

AREA AND EXTENT.

Alaska proper contains an area of 580,107 square miles; the islands of Alexander Archipelago, 31,205 square miles, and the Aleutian Islands, 6,391 square miles. It has an extent of over 1,000 miles from north to south, and the island of Attu of the Aleutian group is 2,000 miles west of Sitka. The longitude of Attu is as many degrees west of San Francisco as Eastport, Maine, is degrees east. The sun never goes down upon the domain of the United States.

JUNEAU.

Juneau, the metropolis of Alaska, is the outfitting point, not only for the great mining district of south-eastern Alaska, but for miners on their way to the Yukon gold-fields. The past year has witnessed a great improvement in the town and Juneau to-day has the appearance of a progressive city with fine buildings, substantial wharves, electric lights, water works, hotels, numerous retail and wholesale outfitting establishments. It is the headquarters of several steamboat lines. The city hall and courthouse stand guard over all on the crest of a high mound seemingly formed for the purpose. From the deck of incoming steamers up Gastineau Channel the view is a pleasing one, the townsite alone being open to criticism, it having undoubtedly been formed by slides from the high mountains which surround it. It has a decided Alpine appearance. The adjacent mountains retain some snow nearly or quite the whole year and the avalanches that tear down their rugged sides in spring form a spectacle that well repays a visit to this enterprising town. I spent some time trying to photograph one of those slides but was unsuccessful, They occur daily, and at night their rumblings will often awaken one from a sound sleep with the impression that an earthquake is shaking the foundation of the city. Cold but not slumbering glaciers occupy parts of this range, one running almost parallel with it, meeting the ocean at Taku Inlet. So lively does it move oceanward that at times the waters adjacent to Juneau are filled with floating bergs to such an extent as to cause the greatest watchfulness on the part of navigators. Although the pass through which the Taku glacier emerges is some twenty miles from Juneau, I have seen bergs as large as a business block floating near the wharves. The lover of the alpenstock can here find real glaciers and mountains which he could ascend unaided to heights sufficient to break his neck without the assistance of accomplished and expensive guides.

Juneau is the immediate center of an extensive and active mining district. It was founded in the winter of 1880-81, gold having been discovered August 15, 1880, by Joseph Juneau and Richard Harris. The town was first known as Harrisburg; later, as Rockwell; but at a miners' meeting in November, 1881, it was wisely and justly re-christened Juneau in honor of Joseph Juneau. The hills and streams proved so rich in gold that miners from many parts of Alaska and British Columbia hastened to this region, and within the year Juneau became a flourishing and typical mining town with that uneasy, ventursome spirit of gambling prevalent that would have excited the admiration of a forty-niner. Since then it has become the commercial center of Alaska. Capital has developed many mines in its vicinity and the past year has brought more money there than ever before. The coming year will undoubtedly mark an epoch in the history of mining in southern Alaska. The business men are shrewd and active and keep abreast of the times. Juneau supports three weekly papers, all bright, newsy sheets that would be a credit to any city having the advantages of wire and train connections with the rest of the world. They are always well filled with mining and general news concerning Alaska. A business directory of Juneau can be found in another part of this guide.

DOUGLASS ISLAND.

Upon Douglass Island, two miles from Juneau and connected with it by ferry, the famous Treadwell gold mine is located. It has the largest quartz-mill in the world. The ore of this mine is of a low grade but free-milling, the average yield per ton being

$3.40; yet the net profits for the year ending May 15, 1894 amounted to $420,948.86.

The Mexican mine, some half mile below the Treadwell, bids fair to become quite as famous. The new mill just completed on this property is of latest design and reflects great credit upon the superintendent, Mr. Robert J. Duncan, Jr. Mr. Duncan is also superintendent of the Treadwell. The ore of the Mexican is of a higher grade than that of the Treadwell.

GOLD-DUST.

Gold-dust and nuggets are the principal medium of exchange throughout the Yukon basin, but little money being in circulation. Everybody carries gold-scales and so adept does one become in a short time that it takes but little longer to make change than with coin. If a hair-cut is needed the gold-dust is weighed out —seventy-five cents; if a glass of whisky, fifty cents, and so on. Everybody carries a buckskin sack. The established value of gold-dust is seventeen dollars per ounce.

Nuggets of one and two ounces are not uncommon. One was found in Franklin gulch weighing thirty ounces. The gold of the different gulches is readily distinguishable, some being of a light color, worn smooth by the elements, while from others it is rough and of a darker hue.

SALE ON BED-ROCK.

This is a method whereby mining claims are transferred from one to another with the agreement to pay a certain consideration in gold-dust, the gold-dust to be taken from the claim thus transferred. This is known as *sale on bed-rock* and is common throughout the Yukon basin.

MINERS' LAWS.

At present miners' law prevails and it is probably much better adapted to the country in its present condition than a regularly constituted judicial system. There are no long terms of unnecessary imprisonment, no corrupt courts, no costly prolonged legal wrangles to be decided, perhaps, in favor of the wrong. Speedy and impartial justice is dealt out to all free of cost and so effectually that no cases of robbery or murder are on record and the utmost good will and faith are preserved toward all. This state of affairs, however, will not last long. With the influx to be expected in the next few years things must necessarily change. A special judicial district court with unlimited powers should be created, thus avoiding the expense and time of appeals which would necessarily follow a court of limited powers and jurisdiction.

A MODEL FIRM.

The map and half-tones used in this book were made by the engravers, Curtis and Guptill, 614 Second Street, Seattle, Wash., and demonstrate anew the fact that Seattle is up to the times in all branches.

Messrs. Curtis and Guptill have the most complete engraving plant in the Northwest and make a specialty of fine half-tones.

We consider their work equal to any turned out by Chicago or New York firms, and we wish them all the success that their prompt business methods and splendid work desires.

A NEW STEAMBOAT LINE

After March 3rd, 1895, the Steamer *Willapa* will make regular trips between Tacoma, Seattle, Port Townsend and Alaska.

This boat has been entirely refitted with electric lights and steam heat throughout. Capt. Geo. Roberts, formerly captain of the City of Kingston, well and favorably known throughout the Northwest, will be in command. Mr. Geo. H. Lent, superintendent of Cornell Steamboat Co., New York City, will be chief engineer. With such competent men at wheel and throttle, a safe and speedy passage is insured. The *Willapa* will make two trips a month, connecting with the Farallon at Port Townsend for San Francisco. This will doubtless prove the favorite merchants and miners line.